Outreach and Identity: Evangelical Theological Monographs
World Evangelical Fellowship Theological Commission

Series Editor: Bruce J. Nicholls

No. 6   Theology and the Third World Church

Other monographs in this series

Theology & the Third World Church

J. Andrew Kirk

InterVarsity Press
Downers Grove, Illinois 60515
United States of America

The Paternoster Press
Exeter, England

ISBN 0-85364-321-0 (UK)
ISBN 0-87784-892-0 (USA)

InterVarsity Press is the book-publishing division of Inter-Varsity Christian Fellowship, a student movement active on campus at hundreds of universities, colleges and schools of nursing. For information about local and regional activities, write IVCF, 233 Langdon St., Madison, WI 53703.

CANADA: InterVarsity Press, 860 Denison St., Unit 3, Markham, Ontario L3R 4H1, Canada.

AUSTRALIA: Bookhouse Australia, Ltd., P.O. Box 115, Flemington Markets, N.S.W. 2129.

SOUTH AFRICA: Oxford Univ. Press, P.O. Box 1141, Cape Town.

Scriptural quotations, unless otherwise noted, are from the Revised Standard Version of the Bible, copyrighted 1946, 1952, © 1971, 1973. Used by permission.

Cover Photograph: Jim Whitmer

Printed in the United States of America

British Library Cataloguing in Publication Data
Kirk, Andrew
    Theology and the Third World church.
    1. Church and underdeveloped areas.
    I. Title.
    270   BR500.A1

    ISBN 0-85364-321-0

Library of Congress Cataloging in Publication Data
Kirk, J. Andrew.
    Theology and the Third World church.

    (Outreach and identity; no. 6)
    Bibliography: p.
    1. Church and underdeveloped areas. 2. Theology–
Methodology. 3. Theology–Study and teaching.
4. Christianity–Latin American. I. Title. II. Series.
BR115.U6K52   1983   261.8'5   83-8560
ISBN 0-87784-892-0

17	16	15	14	13	12	11	10	9	8	7	6	5	4	3	2	1
95	94	93	92	91	90	89	88	87	86	85	84	83				

Acknowledgments

The publication of this study is largely due to an invitation extended by Bruce Nicholls, executive secretary of the Theological Commission of the World Evangelical Fellowship.[1] Bruce suggested I might write up a more orderly account of some thoughts I had been sharing during various travels in the Third World. The focus on the purpose and task of theology seemed to me the best way of relating some of the apparently diverse themes about which I had been speaking, such as kingdom theology, the challenge of Marxism, the origin and nature of liberation theology, biblical hermeneutics for cross-cultural communication of the gospel, the biblical basis for social ethics, and the relation between church and state.

I am deeply indebted to Mrs. Carol Wilson for wrestling with my handwritten text and reducing it to a neat typewritten form, and to my wife, Gillian, who spent long periods of 1979 and 1980 as a grass widow, coping heroically in my absence with three exceedingly lively youngsters. Without her good will, my extensive journeys would have been impossible.

Foreword

Andrew Kirk has done an excellent piece of work in analyzing the situation of the church in Latin America and, through it, the church in the Third World. It is evident throughout this book that he has made a detailed and penetrating study of many aspects of Latin American life and that he is familiar with the literature in the field he is discussing, namely, theology, as well as with the personalities involved. At the same time, he has also fully identified himself not only with the church as a whole but also with the needs and aspirations, the frustrations and ideals, the demands and agonies of the people of the Third World. At times he comes across as a full-fledged citizen of the Third World whose birth and roots are deeply embedded in Latin American soil and the hearts of its people. So, in spite of his British origin, he writes with a true Latin American's passionate concern and frustrated disgust as he sees the many aspects of this continent's problems. It is especially interesting to notice this when he writes about theological training, not only as it concerns the whole area of Theological Education by Extension, but as it relates to his own experience from the start of his teaching in Buenos Aires.

All of this adds credibility to his assessment and makes his essay a document to be reckoned with seriously. It should not be dismissed as a pamphlet which is the product of circumstances rather than biblically based conviction. Here it should be added that the study itself is the product of a disciplined scholar, a thorough researcher, a serious student of the Scriptures with high respect for its authority in every sense of the term. His intellectual skills have acquainted him with various hermeneutical methods and enabled him to apply them consistently in many articles and other works. He has combined his gifts and his formal training in the strict theological disciplines with a deep-rooted faith and an unquestionable commitment to the evangelistic task as it is presented in the Scriptures.

In his opening analysis of the Third World thinkers as representatives of a Third World style of doing theology at the present, Kirk offers little true criticism of their contributions. Apparently the eloquence with which Gutiérrez, Boff, Segundo and especially Míguez present their case is enough for him not to question them. True, he emphasizes theological methods over theological issues in his essay, but it is precisely at this point that these writers have to be questioned. It is one thing to announce that one intends to have a different starting point for his theological task, and another to produce a satisfactory piece of work, one that answers the many different demands both of the biblical record and of the context where it grows and to which it is addressed. Kirk, however, does not comment either way.

Closely connected with this is his comment on the development from Kant to Hegel and then to Marx. Here the impression is given that the climate created by dialectical philosophy and historical materialism is to be approved as a sound basis for the formulation of theology, particularly in the Third World. Thus, what started as an epistemological problem develops into one that is basically metaphysical because of the metaphysical presuppositions involved.

Kirk's missiological emphasis throughout the book is to be commended for many reasons. It is not simply a theoretical concern but a practical one in light of increasing evidence that the mission of the church is becoming the major issue in this last fifth of the twentieth century. Yet Kirk is breaking new ground as far as the Third World church is concerned since missiology is still the exclusive domain of an elite among its leaders. As a matter of fact, the new theologies—though basically missiologies in their own right—aim primarily to be recognized as theological in nature and thus to show their dogmatic bent.

At the same time, theology in the Third World church is still closely connected with pastoral concerns. It is produced mainly by pastors and for pastors with the warmth of the pastoral task in mind. Of course, there are academicians in the Third World whose high accreditation vouches for their ability to produce theology of distinction; but most of these are pastors themselves, and their theological work is drawn from their experience and applied almost immediately. At any rate, the pastoral dimension is, at best, simply implied in Kirk's work; and in this he does not reflect the total reality of the Third World church in its attempt to accomplish its theological task.

But this is a welcome start in what I hope may be a series of attempts both to describe the situation in the Third World church and to guide its footsteps so that it can truly make meaningful contributions in the theological field for the benefit of the church worldwide.

Pablo E. Pérez
Director, The Evangelistic Institute of Mexico

1

A Personal Pilgrimage

During the first half of 1979, having just returned to Britain after twelve years of theological teaching in Argentina, I was invited to undertake some lecture tours, first in Great Britain, later in South East Asia and, on other occasions, in East, Central and South Africa.

The principal purpose of these tours was to share with Christians in other parts of the world something of the theological and missionary ferment coming out of the Latin American church.

Few today will be unaware of the extraordinary vitality of Latin American church life in its response to the desperate spiritual, economic and political needs of the continent. Though much of what Latin American Christians have said, written and done has been controversial, there can be little doubt that such movements of Christian thought and action as Church Growth, Theological Education by Extension, liberation theology, the Grassroots Communities, the new evangelical theology of mission and pentecostalism have made a considerable impact on nearly every sector of the worldwide church.

Within God's providence the last fifteen to twenty years have given rise to exceptional theological and missionary creativity in

Latin America, which at first almost imperceptibly and later with explosive force influenced considerably Christian attitudes and strategies in almost all the continents. Two examples of this are readily apparent. First, a learned and fairly exclusive theological society was willing to relax its strict criteria of membership in order to incorporate Latin Americans; and, second, the extension (or distance) method of theological training has spread with astonishing speed from insignificant beginnings in Guatemala at the beginning of the 1960s until reaching the point where it promises to be the major form of theological education for the future, not only in the Third World but in the Western world too. At the end of this essay I will explore some of the reasons for this major and highly significant shift of emphasis in theological training methods.

Arriving in Latin America for the first time at the beginning of 1967, I had the enormous good fortune and privilege to be caught up in some of the major discussions which led subsequently, during the 1970s, to the blossoming of new missionary concerns and strategies on the part of Latin American Christians. Instant immersion in the New World (in more senses than one) began for me during language study at Ivan Illich's *Documentation Centre* in Cuernavaca, Mexico. Just before I arrived, Illich had thrown down the gauntlet to the North American Roman Catholic Church in a now-famous article called "The Seamy Side of Charity," in the Jesuit magazine *America*. In this article he performed the almost unthinkable task of seriously questioning the policy of North American churches of pouring missionaries across the Río Grande into the South.

Here was one of the first categorical calls for a moratorium on missionary endeavor, a call which in subsequent years has found increasing echoes among Third World church leaders. The Centre was the first to publish the writings of Colombian priest Camilo Torres, who had been killed in an army ambush early in 1966 while engaged in a guerrilla operation as a recent recruit. Illich was using the Centre at that time to encourage an extensive revision of some of the main values which had undergirded the intellectual attitudes of Western liberals toward social and economic matters. This process led to books such as *The De-schooling of Society,* an imaginative though rather utopian look at alternative educational methods and objectives, and *The Nemesis of Medicine,* a far-reaching critique of Western assumptions in health care. At the same time he and his colleagues were engaged in new ways of looking at Roman Catholic teaching in the light of the aggiornamento of Vatican II and the radicalization of Catholic social teaching as expressed in the encyclical *Populorum Progressio* (1967). In all this they enjoyed the patronage, as it were, of the progressive bishop of Cuernavaca, Monsignor Arceo.

Buenos Aires, my destination, lay at the other end of the Latin American continent, distant from Mexico not only geographically but also culturally. The population of Argentina is about ninety-eight per cent of European descent, in contrast to Mexico's large groups of Indians and Mestizos. The capital, called by one Argentine author "the head of Goliath" because of its immense size in proportion to the rest of the country, clings to the edge of the continent like a limpet to a ship's hull, an outpost of European Latin culture, a curious mixture of Madrid, Paris and Rome. After the German theologian Jürgen Moltmann had paid his first visit to this huge metropolis, he was said to have expressed amazement at finding himself back in Europe so soon! That he was actually in Latin America seemed unreal.

In spite of their cultural heritage, the people of Buenos Aires and the rest of Argentina feel themselves to be very much part of Latin America, in the sense of belonging to a continent which experiences more than its share of suffering. Other Latin Americans criticize Argentina for its exaggerated sense of superiority and ability to provide answers to the critical problems of the rest of the continent. Nevertheless, it is true that the Argentine church has contributed probably more than its share to the contemporary theological melting pot out of which the missionary innovations of the Latin American churches have grown. Buenos Aires, partly because of its library resources and its many publishing houses, was, and remains, one of the foremost centers of theological reflection on the continent in the '60s and '70s. Either residing there or visiting frequently have been people of the stature of José Míguez, Samuel Escobar, Beatriz Melano de Couch, Enrique Dussel, René Padilla, Severino Croatto, Juan Scannone and Juan Luís Segundo. Though by no means of one mind as to the direction theological thought should take, they have all shown themselves to be people of immense creative capacity.

Halfway through 1967 I was thrown to the lions, in that I had to teach New Testament courses in Spanish after less than six months' experience of the language. I began to discover that in this new cultural situation the methods and content of theological teaching current in Europe were not necessarily regarded highly.

My own theological training had taken place in the European university tradition. However, even an extended exposure to biblical criticism left me unconvinced of the validity of many of the theories advanced. I could see at least three good reasons for skepticism. *Intellectually* the theories, even when most plausible, often remained at the level of assumptions based on highly circumstantial evidence, and, at their most incredible, they resembled fantasies spun out of the imaginations of specialists whose careers depended to some extent on their continuing ability to pull new rabbits out of the hat. *Spiritually* they were unsatisfying, for the kind of reconstruction they implied (for example, a risen Jesus without an empty tomb) led inexorably toward increasing skepticism and away from a living faith in a living Lord of history. And *missiologically* they proved totally ineffective in arresting the decline of Christian commitment in Western churches; on the contrary, they probably contributed to its acceleration.

Unconsciously, perhaps, I was already looking for a different way of interpreting and teaching the Scriptures: one which was, if anything, intellectually more rigorous, less dependent on unproven speculation, and certainly more consistent with the spiritual and evangelistic needs of the church. Nevertheless, when I began teaching my first courses in Buenos Aires, I did the only thing I knew how to do at that time. Starting with the Synoptic Problem, I paraded the critical theories and prepared critical responses to them.

Fortunately I ran into serious difficulties. Some of these were purely practical—not much of the available critical literature had been translated into Spanish. But other problems were truly significant. In the first place, Latin culture has never, generally speaking, accorded supreme respect to the superiority of theoretical thought. The pursuit of knowledge for its own sake, such as is demanded by the kind of obscure research undertaken by many of the scholarly fraternity, has never been highly valued. If biblical studies, even in the long term, do not appear to produce practical results in the lives of Christian people, then they are regarded as a wasteful, selfish use of intellectual resources. This attitude toward scholarship is obviously reinforced by the immediate social and political problems of Latin America which cry out for Christian collaboration in their solution. Here the unrelated and often marginal pursuits of scholars appear at once both remote and even exotic, belonging literally to another world. Second, and relating to these factors, the younger generation of Latin American students hold European theologians in much less esteem than did their predecessors. Rather than follow the insights and opinions of those working in situations very different from their own, they seek to discover and produce their own theological discourse as they reflect on the meaning of the biblical message in their context.

A combination of these reasons has led to their disregarding the subtleties of European biblical interpretation and their consequent willingness to look for a more flexible and experimental approach. In a way it is a process which began as an inarticulate desire to rewrite the rules of interpretation for the sake of a new theological venture, and which finished as a highly self-conscious and sophisticated use of hermeneutics in the application of biblical interpretation. In brief, the mid-1960s witnessed among those being educated theologically in Latin America the beginning of a shift away from abstract and detached studies to something more obviously related to everyday life. Much of the content of this study will be devoted to analyzing the reasons for and implications of this shift, as well as trying to assess its positive and negative virtues.

My assessment of what was happening is, of course, the result of considerable hindsight. In 1967 I was hardly aware of the issues later popularized by liberation theology and the new evangelical theology of mission. I did find myself open to a new approach in biblical studies, however, and was stimulated to explore this further through my association with the Latin American Theological Fraternity (founded in 1970) and the Argentine Society of Professors of Sacred Scripture (SAPSE), which from about 1966 onward moved away from a concern with European scholarly interests toward an emphasis on hermeneutics.

This new cultural and social situation set me a challenge which has been with me ever since: to find a more satisfactory answer to the problem of relating theory and practice, belief and action, the academic and the committed pursuits of knowledge. It has dominated my own theological pilgrimage, leading me first into a major study of liberation theology and then to a systematic study of Marxism and its peculiar challenge to the church today.[2] Finally, through membership in an experimental center for interdisciplinary study, the Kairos Community, I became interested in trying to understand current economic theories and practices, particularly in their relationship to Third World development.

The present study fulfills an imperative, but I hope not selfish or private need, to articulate some of the concerns I have picked up during my pilgrimage. Many of these, in one form or another, have been shared through articles or conferences with fellow Christians of diverse theological traditions and cultural backgrounds. Some have been kind or polite enough to express their basic agreement; others have expressed reservations, but always with the courtesy of engaging seriously with the issues, even when my exposition of them may not have been the most lucid. My present intention is that my thoughts here should form a kind of first draft of a larger book, in which there will be space to explore at greater length what may appear at first sight to be rather bald statements. In fact, with the hope of receiving really critical responses, I should prefer to think of these ideas as exploratory and provisional. In keeping with the method, notes will be kept to a minimum. I will include a short bibliography of books which have stimulated me whether or not I agree with them.

This study in monograph form is certainly no more than an outline for an agenda. It is inspired by a Third World way of looking at theology, a tract for the times circulated among interested people for their positive and negative comments.

2

A
Revolution

In recent years we have come to expect some surprising definitions of theology from Latin America. Gustavo Gutiérrez argues that theology today should be supremely "a critical reflection on Christian praxis in the light of the Word."[3] In the preface to the Spanish edition of Jon Sobrino's *Christology at the Crossroads: A Latin American Approach*, the publishers describe liberation theology as "a concrete theology related to daily life and based on both an analysis of various situations and the light of the gospel message."[4] Leonardo Boff, a Brazilian theologian, describes the task of theology as "an attempt to elaborate the whole content of Christian faith from the perspective of the demands of social liberation, which anticipates and mediates the definitive liberation of the Kingdom."[5]

Though Gutiérrez admits that other forms of theological reflection may be necessary, he personally pays little heed to them, insisting that "the theology of liberation offers us . . . a *new way* to do theology."[6] Most other Latin American authors would agree with this assessment. In the first chapter of his book *Liberation of Theology*,[7] Juan Luís Segundo begins by asking himself if "it is possible to differentiate between the attitudes of a theologian of liberation and those of any other theologian." In response to Schillebeeckx's definition of theology as "the application of the divine word to present reality," he says that "a theologian of liberation is someone who begins exactly the other way round. . . . The fundamental difference . . . between an academic theologian and a theologian of liberation, is that the latter feels constrained at every step to put together those disciplines which open up the past with those which explain the present . . . in an attempt to interpret God's word directed to us, here today."

In this new Latin American theological consciousness we hear little of the more classical definitions of theology, particularly those which stress the importance of starting with universal statements about God and the world. Liberation theologians are aware that this may produce misunderstanding and irritation among other theologians who are cast in a more classical mold. José Míguez, after arguing that theology in Latin America must engage directly with political and economic realities, being prepared to borrow phraseology culled from the social sciences, says that "the categories chosen do not merely intend to describe human existence but to shape and transform it. . . . A theology cast in political terms . . . has to grapple with the dynamics of the language it uses. . . . The words it uses belong to a context of militancy. . . . The theologian cannot remain any more above the realm of political options. Latitudinarianism is dead: Latin American theology becomes therefore a militant theology—a partisan theology, perhaps." Having made these somewhat unusual claims for theology, he does not surprise us by stating that "such an option will certainly strike most academic theologians as strange."[8] A little further on he notes the essence of the divide between theology being done in Latin America and the more theoretical approach which has dominated Western theology, at least during the last two hundred years: "While the new Latin American theology is deeply polemical, it is not isolationist. Its spokesmen are aware of the problems raised by this new way of doing theology and are willing to discuss them. But they will refuse to be subject to the academic theology of the West as a sort of *norma normans* to which all theology is accountable. And they will reject a theological debate which proceeds as if abstracted from the total situation in which reflection takes place."[9]

That these statements point to a sizable revolution in the definition and practice of theology I hope will become even clearer as we proceed with our discussion. As with all substantially new concepts and movements, it is difficult to grasp the real significance of what is being done; and because it is easy and less threatening perhaps to dismiss Latin American theology as a momentary extravaganza, as the rather unstable birthpangs of the transition from adolescence to adulthood, I will attempt to describe first some of the underlying reasons for this change of direction. There is no smoke without a fire, no historical event without one or more historical causes. Viewed in retrospect, four main factors, more or less coinciding in time, have helped to provoke this new approach to theology.

The Rise of National Self-awareness

First, the new national consciousness linked to the rapid postwar process of decolonization in Africa and Asia has coincided with two events of enormous importance for former mission churches. The move among Protestants toward the indiginization of churches outside the Western world bore fruit during the 1950s and 1960s. Pastoral, administrative and, to a lesser extent, teaching leadership was placed firmly in the hands of national Christians. Naturally, the fervor of political independence influenced the desire for ecclesiastical independence from former founding denominations. The mother-daughter relationship gave way to sisterhood, at least in the thinking of national Christians. Independence meant autonomy, and autonomy implied responsibility for one's own affairs. The new leadership began to assess the church's calling according to the way they understood the situation and challenge facing their respective countries.

With regard to Roman Catholics, there was a man called John XXIII. Facing the Roman Church toward the swirling currents and movements of the contemporary world, he unexpectedly initiated a process of aggiornamento. One of the many results of the Second Vatican Council (1962-65) was that regional Catholic churches gained more autonomy. This was in keeping with the newly announced principle of collegiality among bishops and between bishops and their clergy. The relative flexibility allowed to Catholic biblical scholars since 1943 (with the publication of the encyclical *Divino Afflanti Spiritu*) and the grappling with contemporary religious and social issues in a spirit of moderation in the Vatican II documents gave Latin American theologians the opportunity to grasp a new initiative and begin to reflect seriously and independently upon Latin American life. The first realization was beginning to dawn that theology did not have to repeat what was said and done in Spain, Germany or the Vatican. After four hundred years of theological embargo, the new freedom was heady indeed.

Latin America, of course, has experienced a historical pattern somewhat different from either Africa's or Asia's. Formal political freedom from the colonial powers, Spain and Portugal, was achieved for Spanish-speaking regions at the beginning of the last century, and for Brazil toward the end of that century. Independence for the majority of people, however, has been more hypothetical than real, for the functioning of a fair democratic system has been impeded largely by internal colonial powers representing the interests of small, upper-middle class cliques. Added to this has been the commercial domination of the whole region by the two great industrial giants of the last two centuries, Britain and the United States of America. In this sense there is little difference between Latin America and those nations of Africa, Asia and the South Pacific who gained their independence at a much later date.

A sense of economic dependence on the Western world and of being dispensable pawns in the cold war struggle between the superpowers led to the coining of the now celebrated term *Third World* at the 1955 Bandung Conference of nonaligned nations. These twin realities, which continue to cause grave problems for underdeveloped nations, set the scene for the church's mission in the non-Western world. The church in the Third World lives in a tension between being theoretically free to manage its own affairs and belonging to nations which are in a sense still economic colonies of the rich, technologically sophisticated nations of East and West. This tension is well illustrated by the economic relations between the older and the younger churches: I refer to the subtle manipulation of beliefs, policies and structures that goes on through the allocation of funds and grants by Western sending agencies.

The reality of economic dependence and its consequences—underdevelopment, stagnation and increasing human misery—is the supremely relevant context in which Third World churches have to decide for themselves what faithfulness to the gospel of Jesus Christ really means. Anger at the way in which present world economic forces operate to the further disadvantage of the already disadvantaged has led thinking Christians to question the role played by modern theology in support of prevalent Western attitudes toward development, progress and modernization. The questioning has led to a critical distancing, a suspicion that the apparently objective claims of theological scholarship obscure a lack of integrity in the theological enterprise—unconscious, perhaps, but nevertheless real. This suspicion leads us to the second reason for the shift in theological interests which we have already noted.

European Ethnocentrism in Traditional Theology
Many Third World people believe that a close analysis of North Atlantic intellectual and cultural life will demonstrate a perhaps hitherto unsuspected ethnocentricity. The civilization which has been cradled in Europe, though producing remarkable monuments to human ingenuity and inventiveness, is nevertheless limited in important ways in comparison with other contemporary civilizations. Enrique Dussel, an Argentine philosopher and historian, has pointed out that Europe's expansion from the fifteenth century onward was largely achieved by superior weaponry and a more ruthless attitude to war. The way in which the conquistadors subjugated the Amerindians of Central and South America hardly lends credence to the view that they had achieved a superior moral order to those engaged in human sacrifice. When the Dutch and British rounded the Cape and sailed into Far-Eastern waters, they found nations at a more advanced stage of commercial development than their own. Dussel has suggested that the modern European consciousness has been shaped by the motto *vinco ergo sum* ("I conquer, therefore I am"). Although the supposed existence of pacific, primitive peoples, who were taught the art of killing and violence

only by marauding Europeans, has been exposed as the imaginative figment of romantic minds, nevertheless it is two "white" nations who today hold the "balance of terror" between them.

Perhaps the present radical questioning of the messianic pretensions of European culture and political lifestyle to possess a special and superior role in the modern world (as witnessed, for example, in the resurgence of Islam as an all-embracing cultural and political phenomenon, equally critical of the West and of Communism) may yet prove to be the most dynamic and significant of all contemporary events.

Late twentieth-century European civilization is clearly on the wane as it struggles to find a purpose and direction for the future. Popularly known today as the "American way of life," its tentacles extend to all corners of the earth in the form of the consumer society. In the process it has inflicted a heavy toll on traditional community values in the non-Western world, leaving in their place glitter without substance. For the values that Western people champion suggest that they have regressed to their childhood, pursuing happiness through the acquisition of ever more toys and gadgets. In the process human values are subjugated to the interests of economic profit, and we are pressed into a life mold of selfish individualism whose deterministic grip we find hard to break. Not surprisingly, this lifestyle is not very attractive to those who realize that, in order to follow it, they would have to deny many of the traditional values enshrined in the custom of the extended family.

Christian theology in the Third World, in order to maintain its integrity and credence, has had to disassociate itself from the values of Western expansionism in all its forms. The "made in Europe" image has had to give way to national industries; hence the efforts by Christian thinkers to design theologies more in keeping with the demands of the home market. This process, let me hasten to add, does not of necessity entail a relativistic approach to the gospel, as some Western Christians sometimes seem to assume. In order to rethink the meaning of the gospel in the midst of different cultural assumptions and different histories (Gutiérrez graphically calls it "the underside of history," because the marching feet trample overhead), Third World theologians have had to look again at the epistemological presuppositions of the long European theological endeavor. This takes us naturally into our third reason for the shift of interests.

The Greek and Roman Bias

Dussel, in a massive exploration of the development of Christian thought from its origin in the New Testament to its flowering in the late medieval period, traces the influence of Greek metaphysical assumptions on Christian theology.[10] Whereas "from Paul's letter to the Thessalonians round about A.D. 51 to the last writings of John at the end of the first century, the way of expressing the metaphysical structures implicit in Christianity is almost exclusively that of Jewish theology, with few Hellenizing influences, . . . after the New Testament . . . Christians . . . discovered the necessity of using the same logical organ [as the Hellenistic world]."[11]

The extent to which the philosophical assumptions of Greek anthropology and the more pragmatic premises behind the Roman system of law have conditioned the development not only of theological thought (most notably in the creeds) but also of the imposing edifice of the post-Constantine church is a matter of considerable controversy. No one doubts, however, that, for good or ill, from the time of the Apologists onward theological discussion took place in the restricted context of the Greco-Roman world, and that this context has enormously conditioned the results obtained. Above all, theology largely accepted the dualism inherent in the division of man into body and spirit, and the world into the ideal and the ephemeral.

Now the point at issue is not the degree of influence exercised by Athens and Rome, but the fact that European theology was shaped by the particular environment in which it was done. The long string of cause and effect has reached to the twentieth century, so that Greek dualism and logic and Roman casuistry can still easily be detected in contemporary European theologizing.

Some Christians may accept a view of divine providence which asserts that the expansion of Christianity predominantly into Europe was intended by God. I suspect, however, that Christians east of the Aegean Sea would loudly dissent. I have heard Indian Christians remind us Westerners that Jerusalem is in the Middle *East,* not the Midwest. So the dominance of Christian thought by the intellectual heritage of Europe must be considered accidental. Those who are the inheritors of a different history will need to return to the pre-European basis of theology: the Judeo-apostolic world view. Just as the theology of the New Testament was hammered out of the Jewish Scriptures in the light of the Christ-event, with no discernible accommodation to non-Jewish philosophies (such as Gnosticism), but speaking nevertheless to the realities of non-Jewish cultural and moral values, so contemporary theology must return to its roots in the Old and New Testaments in order to address the particular concerns of its own context in a fresh way. To do this, it may well have to react strenuously (some would say deliberately overreact) against the two-thousand-year tradition of West European theology. Casting off the stultifying inhibitions of this tradition may be a necessary precondition for hearing the biblical text speak its message anew, though at the same time it should avoid at all cost that inverted snobbery which pretends that the West have got it all wrong.

Charles Taber has reminded us that European theology has largely followed the shifts of successive philosophical schools, right down to the all-too-frequent contemporary adaptations to nineteenth-century positivism and twentieth-century existentialism, structuralism and process philosophy.[12] Apart from the fact that these are also creations of the European tradition of thought and cannot therefore automatically be of much concern to Third World Christians, the question arises whether the real challenge to the gospel, even in the West, comes from the philosophical schools. Marginal debates, like that of *The Myth of God Incarnate,*[13] seem to assume that Christian thinking should be judged primarily by its ability to respond to theoretical problems arising from the eighteenth-century rationalistic view of the universe. This expression of priorities is surprising in light of the fact that Western society is being pulled apart at the seams by political and social tensions which, though less sophisticated, are much more real and vital to human well-being than philosophies spawned by an overindulgent academic elite.

The substantial influence of philosophical and religious world views on social life should not, of course, be underestimated or ignored (witness, for example, the divergent attitudes to development taken by India and China in the last thirty years), but neither should they be viewed in abstraction as isolated and self-substantiating idea systems. Such an approach betrays its origin precisely in Western dualism.

Philosophical Shift in Base from Kant to Hegel

This brings us to our fourth and final reason for the shift in theological concern. The philosophical mentor of much contemporary theology, including a substantial group of European theologians, has changed from Kant to Hegel. The effect of this change, which is particularly noticeable in the theological method and emphases of such men as Moltmann, Gollwitzer and Lochman, can be exaggerated, and as a bald statement it may represent somewhat of an oversimplification. However, there has been a noticeable movement in recent years away from concerns normally associated with idealistic philosophy toward issues which contemplate the vital importance of historical and social forces. Hegel, who may either have been the last in a tradition of idealistic philosophers or the first to dip his toe into the reality of dialectics and materialism, is normally mediated today through the vast impact of that most precocious of all the young Hegelians, Karl Marx.

The changes in Europe have been taking place in the context of the Christian-Marxist dialog. In Latin America, Black South Africa and elsewhere, under the influence of a more "voluntarist," homespun Marxism, they have tended to be less theoretical and esoteric and more passionately engaged.[14]

The Hegelian influence has resulted in a more conscious effort to reflect theologically from a given, analyzed context. In Europe the new theology may not yet have got much beyond the application of theological principles and insights to a wider range of human life than formerly. In Latin America, and elsewhere in the Third World, the actual involvement of Christians in programs of social development and change is made into a first step in the theological process of reflecting on the meaning of the gospel in a particular situation.

In the next two chapters I will discuss in greater depth the implications for the task of doing theology of this relatively recent shift of emphasis away from the European tradition of theology in which reflection proceeds by way of logical deductions from systematically granted premises. In the process, I believe, we will discover a new cluster of theological issues which can only be adequately tackled by a generation of Christian thinkers willing to risk new approaches for the discussion and teaching of theology.

3

Consequences of the Revolution

During the missionary expansion of Western churches three kinds of theology have been exported. For ease of reference we may call them Catholic fundamentalism, Protestant fundamentalism and critical orthodoxy. The first two refer to the doctrinal, moral and institutional orthodoxies which stem from the Counter Reformation in the first instance and the Reformation and evangelical awakenings in the second. These two fundamentalisms have been locked in mortal combat in Latin America ever since the beginning of the Protestant penetration into the continent in the middle of the nineteenth century. They both represent complete theological packages, the one stemming from Latin Europe and the other from the Anglo-Saxon world, particularly in its North American expression.

In each case the respective sending countries maintained a rigid line of control over the beliefs and actions of the younger churches. Deviations from the official positions of the founding fathers were not tolerated, and in both cases, though perhaps more noticeably among the Protestants, the children grew up as the mirror image of their parents. The imposition of prevailing ecclesiastical norms sometimes took on a bizarre and grotesque air of unreality, as in the case of the architectural style of churches and theological institutions. These were often almost exact replicas of similar edifices in England or New England, quite out of harmony with the style of buildings where they were set.

Critical orthodoxy refers to that method of biblical and historical studies which has sprung from the positivistic tradition stemming from the Enlightenment. In its more extreme forms it has adopted a wholly naturalistic view of the world and of man's place in it. In the Third World its influence has been very limited, partly because theological teachers who accept its results belong to churches which are not noticeably growing. However, in the past certain key theological institutions scattered here and there in major cities of the Third World like Buenos Aires, Singapore and Manila have felt some of its effects.

Although interest in the pursuit of critical biblical studies at an academic level is at a low ebb among most Third World theologians, some of its results have distinctly weakened the claim of Christian truth to absolute uniqueness and finality. One of the leading exponents of the critical method in Latin America, Jorge Pixley, wrote a book extolling the virtues of the apparently syncretistic traits of Old Testament theological themes.[15] Others, like Father Kappen of Madras, have taken the view that the plurality of theological perspectives in the Bible allow us to choose those which most closely accord with our contextual understanding and experience of God, even when these may be mediated through non-Christian religions or ideologies.[16] Such a process of selection, of course, enables the interpreter to abandon all the distinctive elements of the biblical message, while still quoting Scripture quite freely.

In spite of the more or less extensive influence of these various imported theologies, Third World theological reflection is, as we have demonstrated, adopting an increasingly critical stance toward them. Two fairly obvious results flow from this new situation. First, the implicit claim to universality on the part of Western theology is denied. Second, Third World theologians have engaged in the important and risky task of searching for new ways to do theology.

Serious charges have been laid against Western theology in recent years; these range from its being culturally conditioned to its being culturally imprisoned and blind, and even to its being syncretistic. Precisely because Third World Christians are more sensitive to their own cultural reality, often being a small minority in a vast, unevangelized mass of people, they are more attuned to the cultural vagaries of much Western-orientated missionary work. René Padilla in his memorable address to the Lausanne Congress on World Evangelization (1974) described much modern evangelism as worldly. By this he meant that the techniques adopted and the message proclaimed owed more to the infiltration of cultural factors than to the norms of biblical revelation.

Within that tradition known as evangelical, there is considerable and even strident debate going on concerning the nature of evangelism and the content of the gospel. The Lausanne Covenant has not foreclosed the issue, for some feel that a sufficiently clear distinction was not drawn between evangelism and social involvement, while others believe that the two were falsely separated, thus distorting the unity in mission which characterizes the biblical message.

In any case, Third World Christians are struggling for the freedom to explore new ways of relating God's revelation as recorded in the Scriptures to the missionary challenge of their particular circumstances. This is a difficult task when the Christian media (both publishing and broadcasting) are communicating a message still largely cast in the categories, thought forms and experiences of the Western churches. I have been amazed and appalled at the quantity of irrelevant and escapist literature which has been translated from English into Spanish and Portuguese and which floods the Christian bookshops in Latin America.

In the recently initiated search for new ways to do theology, Third World Christians have begun to adopt the method known as *contextualization*.[17] Although the word is unimportant (it was adopted, or invented, by the 1970 report of the Theological Education Fund of the W.C.C.),[18] the principle is of vital consequence.

I will have more to say in subsequent chapters about the implications of contextualization. At this stage I will simply try to outline just three of the main issues which keep appearing in its current usage: the relationship between subject and object in biblical interpretation, the problems of cultural relativism in the communication of the gospel, and the relationship between theory and practice in theological reflection. In this chapter I will seek to introduce some aspects of the debate about the first two issues. Then in the next chapter we will look more specifically at the third issue. Of course, I recognize that each of these areas of concern really warrants a book in its own right, a much more in-depth study than we can possibly undertake here.

Biblical Interpretation

Third World Christians generally are dissatisfied with a strongly objectivist approach to the biblical text, the result of both the method and assumptions of critical scholarship. They criticize, for example, the attention given to minute and secondary details of interpretation which are often of dubious worth compared to the importance of hearing the message of the Scriptures whole, the belief that neutrality in interpretation can only be guaranteed when the Bible is treated as if it were no different from other ancient literature, and the failure to isolate and discuss the philosophical and cultural assumptions which underlie the academic study and teaching of biblical subjects.[19]

But what most disturbs Third World Christians, perhaps, is the air of almost total unreality surrounding much biblical scholarship. It seems to exist in a rarefied world of its own, unrelated to the need of the general Christian public to understand how the Bible applies to their daily lives, which, it is true, are often far removed from those of the scholars themselves. Critical interpretation, as generally understood and practiced, takes place only within the range of a small circle of professionals, whose main concern apparently is to survey critically the opinions of other members of the fraternity, hoping thus to extend or modify former theories. Rarely, if ever, is direct application of the text to the interpreter's life considered to be part of the task of biblical scholarship as such.

Unfortunately, the theoretical approach often leads to stalemate because conflicting interpretations are necessarily left on the level of hypothesis and conjecture. Behind the method stands the assumption that real scholarship proceeds through the interaction of ideas about the text. If biblical interpretation is conceived of in this way, then the university with its bibliographical and microfilm services is obviously the best place to do it. But the claim that this approach is the only one which merits the description of objective, critical and neutral can no longer be sustained. The approach is absolutely riddled with cultural presuppositions about epistemology (how one discovers truth). With the advent of ideological and psychological suspicion as a tool for analyzing epistemologies, the age of innocence for critical scholarship is coming to an end.[20] Perhaps this is why some biblical scholars in the West are themselves dissatisfied with the general drift of their profession. Brevard Childs sums up this feeling when he says that "the historical critical method increasingly offers diminishing returns for a serious understanding of the Bible within the Church. The method . . . has [not] provided a link between the Church and the world by which the Gospel can be more effectively proclaimed."[21]

The scholarly pursuit of biblical interpretation has not, I believe, paid sufficient attention to two significant issues: the interpreter's position and the problem of communication.

The Sitz im Leben *of the interpreter.* Under consideration here is the status and role of the interpreter. Carefully worked out academic standards and accreditation have defined the status of biblical scholars within the academic community of the West. Within Western consciousness there is a certain mystique of scholarship: advanced degrees and learned tomes are taken to demonstrate expertise. Our sense of achievement and our ambitions are flattered by being the world's leading expert in some field—however remote or narrow it may be.

The mystique is related to the modern syndrome concerning scientific objectivity and the belief, however questionable, that theology shares the prestige enjoyed by scientific methodology. Actually this mystique is declining, at least in the social sciences. In the field of economics, for example, the greater the scientific precision (through the use of complicated mathematical formulas), the further from actual life the studies seem to be. The reason for this is simply that the models used (for ease of discussion) are abstracted from reality. Even lay people know that, although economics is a proper discipline of academic research, economic problems cannot be studied in isolation from human relationships and decisions, neither of which are easily susceptible to laboratory methods of control, analysis and prediction. Personal observation and insight are indispensable factors in any field research, but these can be enormously affected by subjective conditionings.

Therefore the interpreter has to define his or her role and task carefully in relation to the academic community and to the people of God. He claims to belong to both. Sometimes his participation in both may lead to conflict, particularly in terms of his fundamental motivation: is his main concern to use his expertise to help lay Christians be better witnesses to Jesus Christ? Or is it, though not consciously expressed, to defend and advance his academic career? The pressures to conform to a particular code of practice in order to gain a certain prestige are very real. But the point at issue is that the interpreter's understanding of his role will eventually affect his way of reading the Scriptures. There is no academic immunity to this fact.

Another question whose implications biblical scholars do not always face is this: how willing are they to allow the biblical text to be the subject and themselves the object of their interaction? The answer to this question will depend ultimately on the status they accord the text as mediator of God's will. This in turn will depend on the factors, often very subjective, which have caused them to identify with a particular theological heritage in the first place.

A final question concerns biblical interpreters' whole range of activities. Are they primarily involved as partners in the church's missionary task, or are they wholly absorbed by their lecturing and writing commitments? In a Third World situation, both for practical reasons and out of conviction, the possibility of a dichotomy between these two could hardly arise. Biblical interpretation arises naturally out of pastoral and missionary imperatives; it simply cannot be conceived of as an end in itself. Biblical interpretation is primarily functional—and therefore hermeneutical. But the case is quite different for most First World theologians.

The question of communication. One of the principal concerns of biblical scholarship is to discover the original meaning of the text, to know the author's intention. According to current practice, this task demands that scholars observe certain well-defined rules which help them identify several strands of interpretation. These rules allow interpreters to perform their task solely in a personal relationship to the text.

In this search for the original meaning, however, new possibilities arise when it is recognized that interpretation cannot stop at this personal relationship, for what has been discovered has to be also communicated to people who may not be scholars or in any way theologically literate. How far then are biblical scholars involved in the communication of this original sense of Scripture across cultures? Or does their ability to communicate depend on the receptors' being able and willing to adopt their cultural and intellectual premises?

These questions are not only about the mediation between critical scholarship and a particular cultural milieu, but also about how the meaning of texts can be verified. How we see the relationship between the original sense and its signification, or implication for subsequent generations, already determines our methodology. If we believe, as Third World Christians generally do, that it is as important to hear the text as to study it, and that its meaning must be tested not only by the academic community but more importantly by those who are at the frontier of the church's mission, then our understanding of what the Bible says will differ substantially from those who do not share these beliefs.

Those in the field, as it were, are more inclined to test the truth of theological statements by their missiological effectiveness than by their internal logic or their plausibility to the so-called modern mind. If our first consideration is to approach the text as a subject which addresses us with a unique message, then its missiological bearing (its prophetic, evangelistic and diaconic implication) is bound to be the key to any real understanding.

Cultural Relativism in the Communication of the Gospel

The missionary movement has in recent years been subjected to a sophisticated discussion of its theories and practices. As a result,

Christians have become more aware of the issues involved in communicating the gospel across cultural boundaries.[22]

Some leading missiologists, like Ralph Winter, have distinguished different types of communication according to the relative cultural distance between the missionary and the receptor. The distance is measured by comparative studies of the components of culture such as language, value systems, customs, religions or ideological beliefs and practices, art forms and economic achievements. Out of this analysis, graded differences in cultural identity or variance are drawn up and converted into communication types on a scale of one to four.[23]

Awareness of the place of cultural knowledge, sensitivity and adaptation which has risen from both experience and disciplined anthropological and sociological studies has stimulated the search for fresh ways of stating the unchanging gospel and for new evangelistic strategies. According to this thinking the main missionary task is to build cultural and linguistic bridges between received theological traditions and the new culture. The missionary endeavors to discover linguistic, structural and symbolic equivalents to the familiar categories so that he may translate the gospel faithfully into a culture largely unaffected by it before.

This procedure is good as far as it goes. It represents an attempt at communication which seeks to learn and serve as well as to give. Insofar as it demonstrates a willingness to accept the achievements and therefore the humanity of those belonging to the receptor culture, it is an improvement on the rather arrogant and insensitive approach of some early missionary strategies. We must continue to give time and effort to cultural and religious dialog, particularly with aggressive world views like Islam and Marxism, but without for a moment diminishing the scandal of the uniqueness of biblical revelation. In spite of the achievements in cultural awareness, the process has not yet gone far enough. It is significant that the cultural translation we have been describing has been pioneered by Western missionaries in an attempt to locate and unblock cultural barriers to worldwide evangelism and church growth. But the Third World side of the spectrum offers a further important factor in the communication of the gospel, namely, the challenge to the

entangle the biblical gospel, prior to its proclama-
encumbrances of his own culture.

crosscultural communication of the gospel thus becomes a threefold critical process. First, we need carefully to assess what the unchanging elements of the gospel are. Evangelism is a meaningful task only if it speaks of a message for the whole world which people by themselves cannot discover. The gospel is set forth in Scripture; it is not invented by humans in order to promote or defend cultural or political ambitions. Nor should it be accommodated to passing fashions in philosophy, psychology (as, for example, to concur that it is mentally harmful to proclaim the reality of guilt), or political and economic theory (such as Marxism). The Christian's first task in evangelism is to discern the biblical dimensions of the gospel as a wholly unique way of salvation in Jesus Christ.

Second, we need to see how this gospel may apply in a pertinent way to people who have accepted beliefs and lifestyles not informed and directed by the gospel. How far does the gospel agree with the culture's expressed values, and how far does it act as a principle of judgment and change?

Third, we need to discern those elements in our understanding, present action and practice of the gospel which are the direct or indirect consequence of our own relative cultural norms. As I have already pointed out, no one can assume an unbiased and undistorted view of the gospel.

When René Padilla said at the Lausanne Congress on World Evangelization that "it cannot be taken for granted that we are all agreed about the Gospel entrusted to us and that all we need now are more efficient methods to communicate it," he was thinking specifically of the tendency in some Christian circles to follow the practice of a highly aggressive consumer society by making the attractions of the gospel as prominent as possible while reducing to a minimum the cost of accepting its demands. The gospel has often been preached in such a way that it becomes both an adjunct to and an upholder of the values of a capitalist society. It has been presented as a way the individual can achieve in full what the consumer society can only give him in part, namely, true and lasting happiness. Far from challenging and transforming the cultural and ideological values of the present generation, this preaching confirms and prolongs his selfishness and individualism. It is not surprising, therefore, that peoples living in the Third World are highly suspicious of too much emphasis on heaven and the future; this has inevitably resulted in withdrawing from a present concern about the sufferings of the poor, the powerless and the underprivileged.

Contemporary theology has an enormous task in responding to the challenge inherent in the crosscultural communication of the gospel. I would offer the following suggestions as guidelines for further thought and action.

1. *The gospel enters every culture as something new and challenging.* It proclaims Christ's lordship over the whole of life. This may represent great changes in society, as it did in Ephesus when the silversmiths saw their livelihood threatened by the growing numbers of men and women committed to Jesus Christ.

The gospel demands its own set of loyalties. It speaks about many sensitive human issues, such as sexual relationships, the family, distribution of wealth, the exercise of public office, human rights and work. Loyalty to Jesus Christ means opposing every form of injustice, some of which, like manifestations of supposed racial or ethnic superiority, may be inherent to a given culture. And loyalty to Christ may not coincide with loyalty to missionaries whose traditions and customs have not been brought under the judgment of the gospel.

2. *The gospel does not conflict with culture as such.* Culture comes from peoples' creating different customs, systems, values and structures. Man is a creator with a wide range of gifts. Originally man was beautifully and wisely fashioned by God. Now he is a rebellious creature, and the conflict with his Creator, seen as a passion to magnify his own exploits, adversely affects his efforts to build a civilization. Nevertheless, the prophets explicitly tell us that at the end of time "the wealth of nations" will be taken into the Holy City, the New Jerusalem; only what is impure in human culture will be kept out.

3. *Some cultures will be more affected by the gospel than others.* The basic values of a people are usually enshrined in their laws

(witness, for example, the laws on the death penalty, abortion, divorce, sex equality and trial by jury in the Western nations). And these laws show how every culture contains both positive and negative aspects. There is no absolutely Christian culture in existence. The danger of all cultures is to be unaware of their own blind spots, and that of Christians to equate the values of their culture with the teaching of Jesus Christ and his apostles.

4. *Western culture per se cannot be equated with Christian culture.* During the modern missionary movement from the West, however, evangelizing has often been confused with civilizing. This process has been linked to a conscious feeling of cultural if not racial superiority. There are, I believe, two sides to this question.

On the one hand, missionaries have tended to measure social progress in narrowly economic and material terms, thus giving the Western nations an obvious advantage. At the same time they have tended not to appreciate alternative attitudes toward wealth and development. Thus they have shown themselves to be uncritical heirs to a civilization which, because of its aggressiveness and self-confidence, has failed to discern the meaning and importance of values in other cultures, such as tribal solidarity and the art of enjoying leisure—often mistaking the latter for laziness.

On the other hand, however, the prolonged impact of the gospel on the Western nations has brought about a fundamentally positive attitude to certain human values. The most important of these would be individual civil liberties and the conviction that all humans are equal. It may take time before Third World Christians can appreciate that the gospel has made a profound positive impact on Western society in certain areas of life, for they themselves have suffered a good deal from the denial of gospel values. They too have the task of struggling to implement the values of the kingdom in their situation, resisting where necessary every aspect of today's "global village" which destroys or neutralizes those values.

5. *It is important to distinguish between dominant and minority cultures within nations.* Homogeneous societies hardly exist anymore, for colonialism in the last two centuries and the increasing refugee problem of this century have created arbitrary and artificial multiracial societies. The resulting tensions between peoples of

different languages, beliefs and color are enormous and explosive. When minorities feel threatened, they either become exaggeratedly oversensitive and aggressive or they withdraw into defensive ghettos. In both cases the Christian needs to communicate the gospel with compassion, being ready to protect the rights of minorities.

Lifestyles produced by considerable income differentials and accentuated by the greed of the already affluent also produce their own particular cultures. Sociologists speak, for example, of the culture of poverty and the culture of survival. Thus for those who live with the acute malnutrition which affects a quarter of the world's population, all values of behavior will be made to subserve the supreme task of keeping alive and free from disease. Communication of the gospel to people living within the culture of poverty is no theoretical matter. The medium is indeed the message in this case, and the evangelist's lifestyle will have to reflect that of those he lives among; if not, the "good news" *will be heard* as "bad news."

Theology, as it seeks to respond to the complex issue of contextualization, must try to be alert to all the problems involved. On the one hand theologians can no longer carry on their craft independently of the great ethical issues which threaten to annihilate what may remain of man's humanness. The idea, for example, that systematic theology can be pursued as a subject in its own right, independent of the concrete threats which make a human future for mankind increasingly problematic, shows just how far some theology has been conditioned culturally.

On the other hand, theologians, thoroughly aware of the cultural traps into which unwittingly they may fall, must also challenge every attempt to promote anthropological empiricism, as a way of avoiding value judgments about different cultures. Culture is not right just because it is local. Exchanging the absolutist pretensions of Western cultures for the total autonomy of non-Western ones fails to take seriously both the universal and particular implications of Christ's lordship.

The task of distinguishing positive, creative additions to universal human culture from apostate expressions is a continuing one for theology in permanent dialog with other relevant disciplines. Needless to say, it will never be an easy task.

4

Some Essential Conditions for Christian Theology

I have tried to clarify some of the reasons why the church's permanent calling to reflect theologically on its mission is now, as never before, in a period of transition and change. I want to suggest in outline some of the features which I believe a theology for the late twentieth century should possess.

Gutiérrez, in his celebrated book, *A Theology of Liberation*, describes three types of theology: theology as wisdom, theology as rational knowledge and theology as critical reflection on praxis. He is thinking of the time-honored traditions of theological reflection within the church. But if we turn to contemporary theology, a different kind of typology suggests itself. First, there is the systematic study of historical texts, whether these be the Scriptures or the writings of the church fathers, the Reformers or more recent theologians. Second, there is the study of the Christian religion in its different manifestations as a religious phenomenon. In this kind of study, the anthropological and sociological aspects of Christian faith in its institutional forms are central: for example, its impact on the society in which it has taken root, and its success or failure to grow in given situations. It is natural that a phenomenological approach to theology should be pursued in those areas (like Africa and Asia) where other religious traditions have formed the prevailing cultural patterns of life. Third, there is the view that theological reflection must take as its starting point the experience of living Christian communities, exposing this to both the Scriptures and the lessons of church history for orientation and correction.

The first two ways of doing theology can be pursued in complete isolation from the life of the church. They can be and often are the theoretical pursuit of knowledge for its own sake. Those engaged in this type of study, particularly if they teach in a state system of education (university theological faculties) do not need to be committed to the Christian tradition, except perhaps as an interesting and important cultural and historical phenomenon. The third type of theology, however, is deliberately and unashamedly committed to the truth and relevance of the biblical gospel. It is theology done from within the Christian community in its desire to witness both to God's judgment and to his grace operating for the whole of humanity. It believes that ultimately uncommitted, "neutral" theology is a will-o'-the-wisp, because those who try to separate theological thinking from the daily life of the church have already committed themselves to a particular (albeit different) theological, not to say ideological, stance. I am firmly convinced that only this third type of theology, which naturally must feed on biblical, historical and contemporary studies, has any right to be called Christian theology.

In the light of the essential nature of Christian revelation and of current theological discussions going on in Third World churches, it would seem that real Christian theology can flourish, only if the following commitments are made.

We Must Be Committed to Jesus Christ

The historical and living Christ is the center of all theological discussion. Paul Tillich once said that theology is done as a constant interaction between the absolutely universal and the absolutely concrete. These two came together uniquely in the Word made flesh.

But Jesus Christ is not primarily an object of historical research.

We don't really understand him if we rest content with tracing the origin and meaning of the titles attributed to him in the New Testament, although such an exercise is important in establishing the foundations for considering him totally unique. Our ultimate approach to Jesus Christ must be as to the one who has a total right to exercise authority over human beings. To know and understand Jesus fully it is necessary to confess him as Lord of all life, both personal and social.

Jesus is the one who has taken the initiative to find us where we are. Our relationship to him is the result of what he has done for us. This is expressed very powerfully in two sayings from John's Gospel: "You did not choose me, but I chose you and appointed you that you should go and bear fruit" (Jn 15:16), and "You call me Teacher and Lord; and you are right, for so I am" (Jn 13:13). All those engaged in theological reflection must continually face these far-reaching practical claims of Jesus Christ. It is impossible to be uncommitted, for an evasive response is a definite response, nonetheless.

Some have tried to sidestep the issue by dissecting the text to discover whether these or other words attributed to Jesus were ever actually spoken by him. Quite apart from the fact that the criteria used for distinguishing the ipsissima verba from interpolations are often arbitrary and circular, the authority of Christ and his teaching are inextricably bound up with the gift of the Holy Spirit to lead the apostles into *all* truth. The Holy Spirit "will not speak on his own authority, but whatever he hears he will speak" (Jn 16:13). Therefore there is no justifiable way of driving a wedge between Christ's understanding of himself and his mission, and that of the apostolic church. Such an attempt is often a subtle intellectual subterfuge designed to allow us to choose between supposedly conflicting views of Jesus Christ. In this way, by making us the ones who decide which Jesus we will follow, we neatly reverse that relationship to him in which he is the subject and we the object of his call.

The new attempts to reflect Christologically from within Latin America are far removed from this kind of theoretical debate. The search for Christ is not undertaken with the desire to produce a Latin American Christology as such. The object is to regain an authentically liberating Christ in a situation where the popular images of Christ (as either vanquished and helpless, or celestial monarch and remote) are easily manipulated by conservative forces, fanatically opposed to any change in society's present balance of power.

The task of Christological reflection in Latin America, and I would imagine in other parts of the Third World, is essentially hermeneutical: How should one read the New Testament from the perspective of a forlorn and suffering humanity?

In most of the current attempts at systematic reflection, and particularly in Jon Sobrino's study *Christology at the Crossroads*, the emphasis has fallen on the historical Jesus and on functional language about him, rather than on the Christ of faith and the language concerning essences of the later creeds. Sobrino expresses his reasons for this approach in the following paragraph:

> When we stress the historical Jesus, we are underlining his importance as the definitive example of sonship. That example has quite enough concrete details: he proclaims the coming utopia; he denounces injustice as the epitome of sin; he shows partiality towards the oppressed; he unmasks alienating religious mechanisms. And he does all this so that his Spirit will not remain vague and that His God the Father will not remain abstract and manipulable.[24]

If Christological reflection starts from the historical Jesus, then we have a real fundamental content to control our understanding of who Jesus is and was. Christ, as Sobrino states, is not abstract and impartial, but concrete and particular. His universal significance is measured by the transforming praxis of his own ministry. It follows too that, if the contours of this ministry cannot be recovered as historical fact, we have no real starting point for discovering how God acts in the world.

At the center of Jesus' whole life was the kingdom of God. He was the Messiah-King who not only preached its coming but actually inaugurated it, inviting men and women to join him by entering it. The coming of the kingdom brought with it a crisis which faced Jew, Greek and Roman in different ways. The crisis implied a call to both conversion and a liberating praxis in line with the reality of the kingdom as God's new order breaking into the old one dominated by sin, the law, disease and death. Jesus stressed that there is no access to God apart from access to the kingdom, that is, apart from God's action and call to a new way of living. This kingdom is inseparably bound up with Jesus the Messiah.

Commitment to Jesus Christ is commitment to the one who preached, lived, suffered and rose again so that the kingdom might become a tangible reality in the world. Christian theology can only be done by those who, as disciples of this Jesus, are witnesses, agents and evidence of the kingdom—the central theme of God's drama. "We are trying to attain," says Sobrino, "an understanding of Jesus based on a praxis that follows Jesus in proclaiming the coming of the Kingdom, in denouncing injustice, and in realising that Kingdom in real life, even if only partially. That, in turn, will lead to a new round of discipleship."[25]

We Must Be Committed to Change
The kingdom of God is an eschatological event in the sense that God's final purpose to create all things new, abolishing sin, suffering, sorrow and death, is already a reality in the ministry of Jesus Christ and the life of the early church.

The kingdom breaks onto the world scene as a new creative power in the midst of an order of decay, deceit and disruption. As a pointer to the fulfillment of God's will on earth "as it is in heaven," it implies judgment on a world deliberately out of tune with its Creator. Jesus himself unflinchingly confronted the vested interests of power and privilege in both church and state. He showed a radically different approach to human relationships in society: the first would be last; the greatest would be servants; the mighty would be deposed from their thrones and the lowly lifted up; the rich would be sent away empty and the hungry filled with good things.

The kingdom spells out a tension between real but limited change now and total change in the future. This eschatological tension between realism and hope is in itself a powerful challenge to be committed to change. What exists today does not conform to what will be when God puts all Christ's enemies under his feet (1 Cor

15:25). Christ's disciples, therefore, those who have accepted his yoke for themselves, cannot rest content with a situation in which Christ's lordship is not recognized and made concrete. The tension of the kingdom is a powerful spur to bring about change in society.

The Christian disciple's commitment to change is *not*, however, an arbitrary act of nihilism. He or she does not believe necessarily in the total replacement of existing social structures, although the conditions of some societies are hardly worth preserving (as was certainly true in Nicaragua when Somoza was in power, and is probably true of any country where a ruthless dictator is in control). A policy of total revolution implies a trust in human capacity to shape a better future, a trust which is hardly warranted by the achievements of past revolutions. Changes have certainly been made, often they have been dramatic (as in China and Cuba), but always at the cost of great suffering for a considerable number of innocent people. The Christian, therefore, must strive for changes in the system which will genuinely reflect the reality of the kingdom, both in the process and in the effects of the changes.

Dom Helder Camara, as committed as anyone to removing unjust and brutal conditions of life says, "As far as I am concerned, the end can never justify the means."[26] Changes, however dramatic and extensive they may be, if they are achieved by means which contradict the principles of the kingdom, do not produce anything substantially better. The differences of the new order may appear spectacular, but they will prove in the long run to be only superficial. This is why Christians have always insisted that revolutions, unaccompanied by a deep inward transformation of people by God's Spirit, are nothing more than political eruptions. The new man is born from above, not simply out of the negation of the past.

If Christians are deeply enough committed to the transformation of people in such a way that society becomes more like the kingdom, they may well face suffering. Christian believers in places like South Africa and Guatemala are finding that active involvement in promoting a new kind of society brings them face to face with misunderstanding, ostracism, imprisonment, violence and even death. The history of Christian martyrdom is long, though not for that reason any easier to bear. However, taking the consequences for what Helder Camara calls aggressive nonviolence and Yoder calls noncooperation with human laws which violate God's law may well provide that new element in the situation which alone can unblock the logjam of resistance to change.

Theology done from within a commitment to change for the sake of the kingdom has an important tactical role to play. In confrontation with arrogant power complexes it may show how, for example, God's Word is applicable to particular cases of human-rights violations and what are the marks of a genuinely human use of power. In any ensuing period of suffering and grief its role will be that of a theodicy, explaining why submitting to violence is a necessary part of God's plan to bring in a new world (Acts 14:22). Theology can also aid in the search for meaningful, positive and lasting change. In each of these three areas it will have some creative, and perhaps unusual, work to do. If it is true Christian theology, it should be in its element.

We Must Be Committed to the Whole People of God

Encouraging and enabling God's special people to carry out Christ's commission in and for the world seems to me to be theology's fundamental raison d'être. If conscientiously carried out, this task would also prove highly subversive of most traditional ways of doing theology.

The main problem with theology in the West is that it has fallen into the hands of a professional elite who guard their citadel with great jealousy. We are faced with a situation of theological imperialism where only those accredited by the club are permitted to decide theological curricula and theological competence.

Unfortunately, the church has allowed the so-called experts to get away with their restrictive and oligopolistic practices. Few have yet raised their voices in protest against this "priesthood of all professors." And yet, if a man or woman is being trained theologically to serve the mission of the church, why should not the church, the assembled Christian community, have a say in decisions concerning what should be taught, how and where? A centralized teaching authority, unaccountable to the general Christian community, is incompatible with the body metaphor for the church.

If God's people are going not only to benefit directly from theological reflection but also participate in its pursuit, then a fundamental shift of emphasis and method will be required. Theology will be the outcome of Christians engaging in debate about the meaning of their faith in relation to their daily lives. Of course they will need the support of specialists and experienced Christian thinkers to aid them in their search for authentically Christian attitudes and praxis. But such support—theology's indispensable role —will be only one part of an inclusive learning process.

As I see it, the concrete call to be engaged in the *missio Dei* should be the central focal point for all Christian thought. Theology will take its place in this process, but only as one among many other disciplines which, interacting together, will seek to produce committed Christian thought and action in response to Christ's commission to be his witnesses. In this way theology will become the prerogative of every Christian, who will contribute his or her own special expertise, insights and experience to the task of understanding, declaring and obeying God's Word in his world.

Theology will come then into its own, recovering both divine and human purpose. Christians will be able to expropriate for themselves the riches of a theological heritage which rightly belongs to them as members of Christ's body. Henceforth, theology will fulfill its destiny as missiology; it will need no other justification.

As stated elsewhere: "The aim of theology is not just to give a more adequate explanation of things [than do rival systems]. It is an intellectual and pastoral discipline to be put at the service of a Cause. The basic purpose of theology is denied whenever it becomes a mere academic pursuit. Its purpose is lost when it ceases to be a personal and community commitment to a transforming mission in history."[27] With varying degrees of success Third World Christians are attempting to make theology into a liberating instrument in repressive, conflict-riddled societies. They passionately call on theologians in the West to pursue theological research and thinking with the same aim in mind. Perhaps on their willingness to reconsider the purpose and method of theology will depend the churches' ability, at least in Western Europe, to become once again a dynamic evangelistic, prophetic instrument in God's hands.

5

Implications for Theological Education

Third World Christians are not only challenging the theologically literate of the Western world to embark on a theological discussion more engaged with the changing realities of daily life, but they are also questioning the assumptions which have dominated theological education for at least the last one hundred fifty years. The challenge to discover new models of theological thinking implies a change in current patterns of training. The argument is equally true in reverse: different ways of training call for different approaches to theological discussion.

Ross Kinsler, generally acknowledged to be the father of Theological Education by Extension (TEE), makes the following significant statement:

The renewal of the ministry calls for new structures and a new vision. In an intellectual way most churches affirm that the ministry is the responsibility of all the people of God, but in practice they continue to invest most of their resources in the training and support of full time professionals and to depend on them to direct all activities locally and throughout their hierarchies. This is as true of congregational and reformed as it is of episcopal churches. And the recent growth of extension training is in danger of being "domesticated" by limiting it to the "laity" or to churches that cannot afford residential training or to lower academic levels or to "auxiliary" clergy. *What is needed is a new ecclesiology in which the people and their local leaders are in fact the primary base of ministry.* [28]

One might add that what is needed is obedience in practice to the New Testament shape of the church. The problem of ministry and training is not so much the lack of new theories as their implementation.

Churches of a reformed, evangelical or anabaptist tradition have never, perhaps, displayed such a divorce between theory and practice as in the way their ministry functions. Experience seems to demonstrate that the full ministry of Christ's body (often called every-member ministry) will never flourish until the clerical stranglehold on local churches is removed. Local churches will have to be directed by nonstipendiary leaders. Full-time leaders could then devote themselves to specialist back-up ministries on a regional basis. Bishops (or their equivalents) would work with a team whose main task would be to support, strengthen, advise and enable the ministry of the local churches and local Christians to fulfill God's mission in the world. Such a resource team would be somewhat equivalent to the apostolic band of New Testament times. Only in this way could a workable, meaningful, coherent and thorough program of training be carried out effectively, replacing the haphazard and often rather amateur attempts being made at present.

A theological understanding and reorganization of the ministry are not subjects I can pursue here, although they are very important in determining models of ministerial training. The dominant patterns which Ross Kinsler mentions have their logic. They are based on a view of ministry which, in one form or another, has been with us from the second century onward. This view implicitly or explicitly divides Christians into two categories, pastors (clergy) and laity. It reserves the ultimate right of leadership and decision making to only one of the two groups, the minority one. Training is envisaged in conformity with this view of ministry, even when in theory it is repudiated. Instead of a divinely given division of labor being operative within local congregations, with gifts being recognized and encouraged as a corporate responsibility, the minister (see how our language betrays our attitudes!) is taught the rudiments and techniques of a wide range of ministries, many of which (for example, preaching, pastoral counseling, youth work, chairing meetings) members of his congregation can, or could, do better than he. The system leads to frustrations all around, and in many churches it impedes *sustained* growth. The whole process is misconceived. Honesty, however painful, should lead us to a radical (root and branch) reappraisal of the harm our present training patterns are causing to the well-being of Christ's body.

Traditional Theological Education

Emilio Castro, until recently the director of the Commission on World Mission and Evangelism of the W.C.C., has wisely said that methods of theological education will depend almost exclusively on the answer we give to two basic questions: where? and for what?

Where? According to the generally accepted practice of almost every church, proper theological training can only be acquired in the context of a university, theological college or seminary. Such training emphasizes the benefit of extensive periods of residence. People pursuing the same career can learn to live in close proximity to their fellow human beings. They can enjoy a disciplined life of worship together and share more fully ideas on theological and other issues connected with their future work.

In practice, training has concentrated on the need to reach a certain intellectual excellence, measured largely in terms of the ability to pass exams (although an exception is often made for older students). Learning tends to be a process of conceptual input; facts and theories are learned according to a curriculum designed by a central church or university body. When the exams are past, much of what has been learned is unfortunately left behind in the library and lecture room. When the student finds himself subsequently in a local church situation, he does not draw on his academic training in theology; rather he begins a new, often improvised, system of learning. Such a progression results naturally from the method adopted. Postordination training, where it exists, is dogged by it.

The logic of this method is founded on the view that theological reflection is fundamentally the rational interpretation of historical texts. It is first built up into an abstract body of knowledge, and then it is disgorged as a set of principles which can be applied to any given circumstances.

I do not wish to repeat the reasons why I find this concept of theology unreal and even naive, but I would add one further observation particularly relevant to the church's failure in West Europe to engage in an effective mission among substantial sectors of the population. Residential and academically oriented training is elitist and culture-bound. It is only really open to people who have succeeded in a particular educational system by conforming to the expectations of that system's controllers. Those who do not respond favorably to the present norms of literary study and aural learning, or who find difficulty in expressing themselves articulately, will be unable to fulfill present training requirements. This means that the leadership of the church inevitably falls into the hands of people formed within one cultural and intellectual mold. Middle-class educational methods and expectations reinforce a middle-class church, which then produces a future leadership steeped in middle-class assumptions. No wonder the sending nations consider that the church belongs to "them" and not to the national believers. Of course it does. And its training methods will ensure that the same patterns continue.

For what? Theological education as presently conceived works on the assumption that it is preparing men and women for the "professional" job of leadership within the church. Many theological educators are happily committed to this task. Others, however, are troubled by some of the issues we have been raising in this study and feel somewhat confined and coerced by the system. But they believe that meaningful changes can be made from within the present structures. They deserve great encouragement.

There are yet others who find the context of a theological college, seminary or university faculty a good base from which to pursue their own personal theological interests. Their motivation is the pursuit of knowledge for its own sake. Such people may be adept at writing well-researched articles or books, but it is unlikely they will be good educators. The question of whether the pursuit of knowledge for its own sake is a legitimate part of committed theological thinking and training needs, I believe, to be examined much more closely. Does not such a pursuit already betray a particular kind of commitment?

Scholars usually defend this commitment on the ground that only in this way can academic and intellectual freedom be guaranteed. There is some truth in this. Certainly theological educators should not be beholden entirely to the dictates of a centralized ecclesiastical bureaucracy. Educators must be allowed to lead and guide as well as to be led and guided. The most appropriate education and the best theology are not necessarily what the majority may want. Christians in local situations may need their horizons broadened and their imaginations stretched. However, it is doubtful that this is the kind of freedom that many theologians are talking about. What they probably mean, unfortunately, is that private enterprise should be allowed to hold sway in theological institutions so that individuals can maximize their own interests.

One wonders, however, whether this is real Christian freedom. Surely Christian freedom is fundamentally freedom to serve others. In the context of theological education this must mean putting oneself at the disposal of one's fellow Christians. I would suggest that the church does not so much need greater theological freedom for individuals as more theological creativity for the sake of the body. Academic freedom has often led to philosophical and ideological conformism and theological stereotypes. There is every reason to believe that theological creativity is best stimulated when theologians are consciously seeking to contribute to the church's calling to make disciples of all nations. Theology is for the church in its testimony to the world; it is meant to be a servant of the servant of God. Apart from this it has no rationale.

Partly because present training methods have proved inadequate to the contemporary needs of the church, and partly because of a rediscovery of New Testament patterns of ministry, new experiments are under way in many parts of the worldwide church. Many of the new insights have been incorporated into extension (or distance) patterns of training (TEE). We will conclude our discussion, therefore, by looking briefly at some of the benefits of training Christian leadership by extension methods.

Theological Education by Extension

First, theological training is potentially offered to every Christian who wants it. Extension programs effectively narrow the gap between the theologically rich and the theologically poor. They involve Christians actively in their own homespun process of theological reflection as this arises naturally out of the issues they face in witnessing daily to Jesus Christ. They also help to build the confidence of Christians in their ability to train others, rather than being merely the passive recipients of the crumbs which may fall from the pulpit or the church's weekly Bible study. (Although I would not underestimate the value of teaching and sharing together the meaning of Scripture, I believe experience shows that these activities are not very effective vehicles for a coherent training program.)

Second, people are trained during the same twenty-four-hour period in which they have to earn their living and fulfill other aspects of their daily life. They experience a constant natural pressure to relate what they learn to the rest of their waking day. Those who participate in this process will be less like pieces of blotting paper which absorb a stream of facts, than channels who take what they are receiving from tutors and allow it to fill the relevant cracks and crevices of the world they know. Of course, they will need to master given facts and learn to discuss and sift ideas. But this process will never be removed from their need to know how to live more faithfully and fully as Christians. They will strive to appropriate the theology they study for themselves rather than just to learn it as a series of facts. Its overriding purpose will be to form disciples of Jesus rather than to learn information about discipleship.

Third, theological training is envisaged as an ongoing process. Present methods often give the impression, even if unintentional, of a steep uphill climb followed by a plateau. Once exams are past and the student has secured the qualifications for recognition by the church, he is understandably tempted to feel that he has arrived. The temptation is reinforced by the fact that few serious in-service programs are made available to the ordained leader during the rest of his working life. Extension training methods, with their minimal emphasis on academic accreditation and their maximum emphasis on the acquiring of skills, makes the "stop-go" method of training much less likely. If one learns to study, say, the book of Isaiah in order to consider God's calling to the church in a particular situation, then one will receive stimulus to go on studying the text, for as the situation changes, so will the questions which we put to the text. But this encouragement will be absent if we are obliged to study the text in order to pass an exam on what critical scholars say about it. The challenge of a rapidly changing society will be a far greater motivation to permanent study than changes in the critical theories of professional commentators.

Fourth, the context of a heterogeneous rather than homogeneous group will stimulate learning. At a university, theological college or seminary, those studying usually come from a similar social and educational background, are of a similar age (though the percentage of older people taking up full-time Christian service has increased), and are training for the same kind of ministry. None of these things are true in the extension centers. Particularly important, there is the kind of interaction which the group's wide diversity of experiences makes possible. The extension sessions are fascinating experiences in which sharing encourages growth together as the variety of input is considered and its relevance assessed. Of course, heterogeneity does not automatically guarantee comprehensive communication; the art of listening and understanding has to be worked at.

Fifth, as the participants are encouraged to reflect on the gospel's application to their whole lives, so the arbitrary distinction between the experts and ordinary Christian people will tend to become less significant. This is bound to be a long process, as so much education in the past has concentrated on the gathering of facts rather than on their use to confront real issues. The theological educator is undoubtedly needed because his training and accumulated reflection give him unique resources, but the persistent observation of everyday life also provides a valid source of reflection. Pertinent theological thinking is seriously weakened by the absence of either kind of contribution.

Sixth, the purpose and the atmosphere of study will differ a good deal from their counterparts in more traditional types. For one thing the study is not linked to a specific career. Conventional theological education is limited by its nature to a full-time career and must, therefore, prepare a person to fit into the requirements of that career. As a result it is not free to explore the possibilities of adapting training to the challenge of mission. The extension method, in contrast, "deprofessionalizes" theological education and concentrates on giving training according to the specific needs of Christians.

Another important consideration is that the participant does not receive a grant to study (although when the need arises, he may be helped to purchase basic books, texts and study guides). Some may feel that the relationship between theological learning and finance is not important or even relevant; experience, however, would suggest otherwise. Personal observation confirms that motivation and interest in study are sustained more fully among those who pay to take courses than among those paid to do so. A significant parallel might be the Open University courses in Great Britain in that they are both more widely accessible than ordinary university courses and their cost has to be met, in part, from the earnings of the students.

Lesslie Newbigin in a pungent article on theological training suggests that the nonstipendiary ministry should be the norm of ministry in the church and the salaried clergy should be the auxiliaries. This would imply "acceptance of the fact that the *normal* local leadership would be that of non-salaried members of the congregation."[29]

Seventh, in the kind of extension training we have been discussing, those with theological expertise would have to expose themselves to both situations and debates with which they might not be familiar. The biblical scholar could not rest content with a summary of the latest findings in Pauline research or the relationship of the covenant to possible extrabiblical parallels. He will either be forced to work out biblical principles for a wide range of pastoral and ethical questions, or he will have to conclude that he is incapable of communicating his knowledge to the situation in which the majority of his brothers and sisters in Christ lead their daily lives. This openness may be painful to the individual concerned, but it is the beginning of an engaged theology. The problem of the present system is that the theologian can be let off the hook; nothing obliges him to make his study really human and contemporary. He can devote himself to the academic life without ever being forced to face the possibility that he is evading the challenge of using his expertise to help the church fulfill its missionary call.

A critical look at TEE. Taken together, or even separately, these factors spell a fair-sized revolution in our attitude to training for ministry and mission. In practice they substantiate an engaged approach to theological reflection. There are, of course, certain disadvantages and difficulties in this method, although they have often been magnified by those with no practical experience of TEE. We should not, however, try to hide or ignore them.

Up to the present TEE has expended the bulk of its energies on training Christians for church-related ministries rather than on preparing Christians for a faithful, biblical witness in the maelstrom of life outside the church. Sometimes one gets the impression of an enterprise basically designed to perfect the ecclesiastical machine so that its growth may be more streamlined and effective. Such a criticism can, however, be an easy gibe and does not make the necessary distinction between a method and the content of its program. There is nothing inherent in the method which would impede training for pioneer tasks within society. This latter will come about when the largely evangelical constituency which has adopted TEE methods becomes more aware of the total dimensions of the biblical gospel.

Another strong criticism raised by Third World ecumenical leaders concerns the possibility that Western churches, through missionaries, will try to use the new methods to continue their theological and institutional control of the newly independent churches. At a time when the long-established theological institutions are employing an increasing number of national teachers, the advent of TEE has stretched the churches' teaching resources beyond the capacity of national Christians to respond. Consequently, extension training has largely fallen into the hands of expatriate teachers. This includes the writing of the basic texts (programmed and otherwise) on which the whole enterprise is founded.

This is clearly far from an ideal situation, and one of the most urgent needs in mission-church relations is for those who give extensive grants for ministerial training in the Third World to be more ready to trust theological education to national Christians. On reflection, however, this objection to TEE is not substantial, for, as in the case of the first objection, the method itself does not inevitably produce this abuse. As a matter of fact, the method could equally well be used to make people aware of the need to criticize and supplant structures and strategies imported in the colonial and neo-colonial period of missionary work. Moreover, the exchange of nationals for missionary personnel does not guarantee a more contextualized approach to training. Many missionaries, particularly from Europe, in the changed climate of opinion on world mission now champion the cause of local experiment and creativity, while nationals are not always able to break so easily with past traditions. This may be partly due to the missionaries' ability to acquire greater freedom from direct ecclesiastical control than their national brothers; also their lack of permanent status in the church and their category as guests mean that they are more likely to represent innovation than continuity. This is also true, I believe, because positive aspects of church life in the Third World, like TEE and Church Growth, have received good press among the flagging and rather dispirited churches of the West. And this, in its turn, has tended to produce missionary recruits who are frustrated by the inertia of their own home churches, and attracted by the apparent dynamism of the younger churches.

A more forcible objection to extension training in any or all of its forms is that it does not allow sufficient time for concentrated periods of study, leading, perhaps, to the completion of research projects. For this to take place residential and library facilities must be available. Obviously, by its nature, extension training is not geared to sophisticated research projects. If the church considers such concentrated study to be an essential part of its total ministry (and no one should doubt that periods of time for reading, reflection and writing ought to be made available to people with the gifts to profit from them), then it should make funds available to support it. Short residential courses may also be a valuable back-up to the regular extension seminar sessions.

Admitting the great value of residence in these two instances is far from agreeing that residential, full-time training should be the norm. Part of the argument against residential theological training is the amount of time inevitably lost by students (particularly if they are young) because they are unable easily to identify the crucial areas of study. For those who lack experience in the field, study is inevitably a rather hit-or-miss affair. They are also dependent for orientation on theological lecturers whose own practical experience of the churches' front-line mission may be limited. In terms of actual, effective study hours per person, extension training provides a better framework for the maximum use of resources.

Only a rash and ignorant person would deny that extension training methods do have some disadvantages and that, in practice, problems still need ironing out. However, the claim is quite justified that the advantages are much more noteworthy. The most important aspect of this debate from the viewpoint of the arguments of this whole study is the relationship between particular molds of theological thought and corresponding patterns of theological education. What I am advocating is quite simply, though not superficially, new wineskins (methods of training) for new wine (methods of doing theology).

6

Profile of a Theologian for Tomorrow's Church

As far as the task which confronts theology in today's world is concerned, we are clearly living in a period of transition. For reasons I have briefly spelled out in these pages, the old norms are no longer adequate to meet the challenge of a humanity hurtling into the future at an impressive speed, but not certain where it is going. Every year the question marks are growing larger. The old norms, we are discovering, also contradict the way in which the biblical writers related God's revelation to the reality of their day.

Theology can no longer assume, therefore, that the methods by which it has functioned in the recent past are now valid and workable. Indications are that it is faced with one of two options: either to withdraw increasingly into the intimate circle of like-minded colleagues (including nontheological members of the academic fraternity) or to converse passionately with people of every kind as they ply their trades day by day in the marketplace. If theology wishes to be a discipline relevant to more than a tiny minority of the human race (those who are fully paid-up members of the same club), it will have to lose its present academic inhibitions. The system (meaning the academic institutions) will, unfortunately, guarantee the continuance of the old methods and assumptions long past the time they serve a useful purpose to the church in its witness to Jesus Christ. The reason for this is that a huge amount of human and financial capital has been invested in the system, and powerful interests will dedicate themselves to rationalizing its continuing operation.

If, however, theology is going to become a fully conscious agent of mission in ways like those I have suggested, then the context in which it is done will have to become much more diversified than it is at present. Theological thinkers and educators will be wise to become independent of the academic establishment network—so that in the event of these either having to cut back or ceasing to operate (perhaps because of financial stringency), theological education would be unaffected.

Of course, the diversification of context and method will probably broaden the present breach between traditional theological study and the new methods and experiments. This is part of the cost of living in a time of transition and uncertainty. It is unreal to expect that everyone will share the same opinions concerning the future of theology. Many will express (and some already have) their dismay about the trends toward a more contextualized theology. For them this is simply another (perhaps more sophisticated, perhaps more naive) example of relativism and reductionism creeping into Christian thinking. They will have nothing to do with it; or so they think, unaware as they are of their own brands of these things.

In the run-up to the twenty-first century, it is to be hoped that all those who believe they are engaged in committed Christian theology, however they view their task, will maintain their links and continue to talk to one another. Breaking off communication, however great the differences, would be a profoundly unchristian act. Among Christians there should always be a willingness to listen and understand before disagreeing.

No set of unchanging circumstances in which a theologian may ply his craft exists. In the future he may find the context in which he works increasingly unstable and perplexing. Therefore, we cannot predict the way in which theological debate will or ought to go in the years ahead. But, arising out of our discussion, I would offer some tentative ideas about the theologians I believe the church now needs.

First, they will have to be actively in touch with the grassroots of the church. This will mean a conscious effort to cultivate friendships and be involved in fellowship groups outside normal contacts with students. They need to experience and appreciate the fact that most Christians live in a world very different from that of the university, college or seminary. And their concerns and questions are correspondingly different. This makes the theologians' regular, committed involvement in a local church absolutely indispensable, including availability for involvement in extension lay-training programs.

Second, it would be good if they had some regular contact with life outside of the Christian community. This will vary according to the opportunities which each country offers for democratic involvement in society. Living outside the compound, among a good cross section of fairly normal "pagans," would be a realistic vantage point from which to reflect theologically. Opportunities for involvement in local council, action and pressure groups are open to most citizens in most Western nations. In situations of totalitarian government presumably such involvement would be impossible. However, it is also unlikely that those conditions would allow theologians to isolate themselves from the struggles of ordinary people anyway.

Third, theologians must begin to discover the centrality of the hermeneutical task for their thinking. Instead of concentrating almost exclusively on theological texts, they should be well informed about subjects other than their own and learn to relate together the thought worlds and concerns of each. It may well be that they should specialize in another discipline, or at least master enough information so that they can follow the arguments of other specialists. Such subjects as pastoralia, ethics and mission can no longer be an addendum to theology, but must rather become its starting point. Every theologian must be prepared to study and teach subjects where he is obliged to apply his knowledge and understanding of the foundation texts.

Finally, theologians must be willing to cooperate in interdisciplinary study teams. One of the crying shames of the present system of theological education is that committed Christians in all walks of life are receiving little or no systematic help from those with good theological groundwork. Many Christians are engaged in study projects in which they are grappling with the issues and challenges of their own profession, but theologians to help them integrate their faith with their profession are notably absent. This may well be due to the fact that they have not learned the art of interdisciplinary work. Theologians need training in this art. The church would benefit enormously by the multiplication of serious interdisciplinary projects like the Kairos Community in Buenos Aires, the TRACI Community in New Delhi, the Zadok Centre in Canberra, Regent College in Vancouver, New College Berkeley in California and the new London Institute in Great Britain.

The formation of research and action groups of this nature would be one important indication that the church at large and evangelicals in particular are beginning to take seriously the need for a fundamental shift of emphasis on the theological front. Maybe it will be up to lay people to pressurize the leadership from below so that new experiments in theological formation can be speedily put into operation. Our one supreme desire is to act together so that in the most real way possible every thought may be taken captive to obey Christ.

Notes

[1] I should emphasize that the views I express do not represent in whole or in part any official position adopted by the Theological Commission, nor do they necessarily coincide with the opinions of its executive secretary.

[2] J. Andrew Kirk, *Liberation Theology: An Evangelical View from the Third World* (London: Marshall, Morgan and Scott, 1979; Atlanta, Ga.: John Knox Press, 1980).

[3] Gustavo Gutiérrez, *A Theology of Liberation* (Maryknoll, N.Y.: Orbis Books, 1973), p. 13.

[4] Jon Sobrino, *Christology at the Crossroads: A Latin American Approach*, trans. John Drury (Maryknoll, N.Y.: Orbis Books, 1978), p. xi.

[5] Leonardo Boff, *Teología desde el cautiverio* (Bogotá: Indo-American Press Service, 1975), p. 32.

[6] Gutiérrez, *Theology of Liberation*, p. 15; Gutiérrez's emphasis.

[7] Juan Luís Segundo, *Liberation of Theology* (Maryknoll, N.Y.: Orbis Books, 1977).

[8] José Míguez, *Revolutionary Theology Comes of Age* (London: S.P.C.K., 1975), pp. 79-80.

[9] Ibid., p. 86.

[10] Enrique Dussel, *El dualismo en la antropología de la cristiandad: desde el origen del cristianismo hasta antes de la conquista de América* (Buenos Aires: Editorial Guadalupe, 1974).

[11] Ibid., p. 25; my translation.

[12] Charles Taber, "Is There More Than One Way to Do Theology?" *Gospel in Context* 1, no. 1 (January 1978):4-10.

[13] John Hick, ed., *The Myth of God Incarnate* (Philadelphia: Westminster, 1978; London: SCM Press, 1977).

[14] Cf. José Míguez, *Christians and Marxists: The Mutual Challenge to Revolution* (London: Hodder and Stoughton, 1976).

[15] Jorge Pixley, *Pluralismode tradiciones en la religión bíblica* (Buenos Aires: Editorial La Aurora, 1971).

[16] Father Kappen of Madras, unpublished paper delivered to a consulation on liberation theology in Bangalore, June 1979.

[17] Cf. Bruce Nicholls, *Contextualization: A Theology of Gospel and Culture* (Downers Grove, Ill.: InterVarsity Press, 1979; Exeter, England: Paternoster, 1979).

[18] Now it is the Programme for Theological Education (P.T.E.).

[19] A much fuller discussion of this subject will be found in my book *Liberation Theology*.

[20] For the way these work, see Segundo, *Liberation of Theology*. However, it ought to be pointed out that Segundo does not allow the ideological critique sufficient bearing on Marx's theories. Cf. my *Theology Encounters Revolution* (Leicester, England; Downers Grove, Ill.: InterVarsity Press, 1980), chap. 8.

[21] Brevard Childs, "Symposium on Biblical Criticism," *Theology Today* 33, no. 4 (January 1977).

[22] See especially John R. W. Stott and Robert Coote, *Down to Earth: Studies in Christianity and Culture*, 2d ed. (Grand Rapids, Mich.: Eerdmans, 1980).

[23] See "The Highest Priority: Cross-Cultural Evangelism," in J. D. Douglas, ed., *Let*

the Earth Hear His Voice (Minneapolis: World Wide Publ., 1975).

24Sobrino, Christology at the Crossroads, p. xxv.

25Ibid.

26Dom Helder Camara, The Conversions of a Bishop: An Interview with José de Broucker (London: Collins, 1979), p. 199.

27J. Andrew Kirk, "Liberation Theology," Christian Graduate 32, no. 1 (March 1979):26.

28Ross Kinsler, "Ministry by the People," Ministerial Formation (Program on Theological Education) 5 (January 1979):8-9; my emphasis.

29Lesslie Newbigin, "Theological Education in a World Perspective," Churchman 94, no. 2 (1979):110.

Select Bibliography

Anderson, Gerald H. and Stransky, Thomas, eds. *Mission Trends, No. 3: Third World Theologies.* Grand Rapids, Mich.: Eerdmans; Ramsey, N.J.: Paulist Press, 1976.

——————————. *Mission Trends, No. 4: Liberation Theologies.* Grand Rapids, Mich.: Eerdmans; Ramsey, N.J.: Paulist Press, 1979.

Boesak, A. *Farewell to Innocence.* Kampen: Kok, 1977.

Cardenal, Ernesto. *Love in Practice: The Gospel in Solentiname.* Maryknoll, N.Y.: Orbis Books; London: Search Press, 1977.

Childs, Brevard. *Introduction to the Old Testament as Scripture.* London, 1979; Philadelphia: Fortress, 1979.

de Santa Ana, J., ed. *Toward a Church of the Poor.* Geneva: W. C. C., 1979.

England, J. C., ed. *Living Theology in Asia.* London: SCM Press, 1981.

Gill, R. *Theology and Social Structure.* London: Mowbrays, 1977.

Goldingay, John. *Approaches to Old Testament Interpretation.* Leicester, England; Downers Grove, Ill.: InterVarsity Press, 1981.

Gutiérrez, Gustavo. *A Theology of Liberation.* Maryknoll, N.Y.: Orbis Books, 1973.

Hesselgrave, David J. *Theology and Mission.* Grand Rapids, Mich.: Baker, 1978.

Kinsler, F. Ross, ed. *Ministry by the People.* Maryknoll, N.Y.: Orbis Books, 1983.

Kirk, J. Andrew. *Liberation Theology: An Evangelical View from the Third World.* London: Marshall, Morgan and Scott, 1979; Atlanta, Ga.: John Knox Press, 1980.

——————————. *Theology Encounters Revolution.* Leicester, England; Downers Grove, Ill.: InterVarsity Press, 1980.

Koyama, Kosuke. *Three Mile an Hour God.* London: SCM Press, 1979; Maryknoll, N.Y.: Orbis Books, 1980.

Kraft, Charles H. *Christianity in Culture: A Study in Dynamic Biblical Theologizing in Cross-cultural Perspective.* Maryknoll, N.Y.: Orbis Books, 1980.

Lienemann-Perrin, C. *Training for a Relevant Ministry.* Geneva: W. C. C., 1982.

Marshall, I. Howard, ed. *New Testament Interpretation: Essays on Principles and Methods.* Exeter, England: Paternoster Press, 1977; Grand Rapids, Mich.: Eerdmans, 1978.

Míguez, José. *Revolutionary Theology Comes of Age.* London: SPCK, 1975.

Pobee, John S. *Toward an African Theology.* Nashville: Abingdon, 1979.

Shorter, Aylward. *African Christian Theology: Adaptation or Incarnation?* London: Chapman; Maryknoll, N.Y.: Orbis Books, 1977.

Smart, J. D. *The Strange Silence of the Bible in the Church.* London: SCM Press, 1970.

Sobrino, Jon. *Christology at the Crossroads: A Latin American Approach.* Trans. John Drury. Maryknoll, N.Y.: Orbis Books, 1978.

Stott, John R. W., and Coote, Robert. *Down to Earth: Studies in Christianity and Culture.* 2d ed. Grand Rapids, Mich.: Eerdmans, 1980.

Stuhlmacher, Peter. *Historical Criticism and Theological Interpretation of Scripture: Towards a Hermeneutic of Consent.* Philadelphia: Fortress Press, 1977; London: SPCK, 1979.

Torres, Sergio, and Eagleson, John. *The Challenge of Basic Christian Communities.*

Trans. John Drury. Maryknoll, N.Y.: Orbis Books, 1981.

———————. *Theology in the Americas.* Maryknoll, N.Y.: Orbis Books, 1976.

Torres, Sergio, and Fabella, V. *The Emergent Gospel: Theology from the Developing World.* Maryknoll, N.Y.: Orbis Books, 1978.

Vincent, J., ed. *Stirrings: Essays Christian and Radical.* London: Epworth Press, 1976.

Wink, Walter. *The Bible in Human Transformation: Towards a New Paradigm for Biblical Study.* Philadelphia: Fortress Press, 1973.

Winter, D., ed. *Putting Theology to Work.* London: British Council of Churches, 1980.

Winter, Ralph D., ed. *Theological Education by Extension.* Pasadena, Calif.: William Carey Library, 1969.